Can I Touch You: A Collection of Love Poetry
By Synthia SAINT JAMES

ISBN-13: 978-0615579313
ISBN-10: 0615579310

DEDICATION

In GOLDEN light & love

Author's Preface

In 1970, a year after I sold my first paintings, I began writing poetry. For this book I selected from the poetry I wrote between 1970 and 1982.

One of the first times that my poetry was performed by fellow actors was at Inner City Cultural Center in Los Angeles, the performing arts school where I studied acting and dance, in The Stormy Weather Café in 1977 or 1978.

Since that time some of my poetry has been released, as what we now call spoken word on cassettes and on a CD titled *Can I Touch You Love Poems and Affirmations*. I recorded my poems in a studio just outside of Washington, DC and my friend Melba Moore recorded my affirmations in a studio in New Jersey. That was in the early 1990's.

I think that it's long overdue for me to begin to share my poetry again. Hope you enJOY!!!

Chapter One

In and Out of Love

I love hard

make love softly

and hurt badly

I turned twenty-five today

I'm still attractive and desirable

people do pursue me

but one day

I'll be old

for age creeps up on you

I realize it

contend with it

but I must make something of myself

leave my mark never to fade away

never for people to look at me and say

what a beauty she used to be

what a shame

but instead to look at my work

and say she's beautiful

my destiny hopefully

that will be

Feelings have the power

to repeat themselves

bury them as far as you can

deep within

but that certain someone

can easily bring them

to the surface again

Bubbling

I'm bubbling inside

these bubbles make me smile

I'm smiling inside

do you suppose that

people can see

This feeling

I've felt it before

just get carried away

too much of myself

I've given away

the outcome

always the same

I've met you before

but saw you for the first time recently

When you smiled at me

I felt you

in the dark of a crowded room

you were even under a costume

the rest of that night

and each day thereafter

my thoughts fell constantly on you

in just a little time

I was happy to find

that a glow had also

started in you

I could call it love

it feels like love

only time will tell

so I won't call it anything

until I'm sure

I just talked to you

you sounded so good

so good

so good

To think of being with you

is to imagine feeling

comfortable

loved

and lovable

Everyone has a place in time

I hope my place is beside you

Like an epidemic

you have spread

into every fiber

of this

my body

Your voice

the sweetest of sounds to my ears

your smile

the fresh taste of raindrops

your touch

a blanket covering me with warmth

you to me

have come to mean so much

In love once again

was I ever out of it

or was it just stuck behind

something called logic

Feelings pop up to the surface

given heat

and just a little time

in a strange but tender way

you bring me to the surface

You gnawed at my wall

tore it down once again

like always before

me left unguarded once again

but surrounded by your love

I feel warmed by you

you're a warm summer's night

I feel natural and easy with you

once I'm there beside you

a little nervous before

a unique attraction

a feeling of newness

my hope is of many dimensions

of this I'm sure

Like a word

with added suffixes

enables it to describe

you've added something to me

that makes me more creative

I love you

but not selfishly

but like the few who love enough

to just want to see you happy

You're a cozy nest

I'm the captive bird

I love being enveloped by you

you're so warm

and I feel at such ease inside

The day is coming to a close

it's getting dark outside

but because of you

I feel nothing but light

Inside

I feel elated

damn if love isn't funny

one minute crying

the next laughing

Look into my eyes

and you'll see within me

could you love

what you see

The end of one affair

the beginning of another

either you fight becoming attached

or you give it your all

you put too much into it

you may end it quickly

both ways

When I decided not to run again

I left myself wide open

to whatever comes my way

and all the emotions

a big step oh yes

could be scary I guess

but it's a decision I'm going to stick with

Today I feel love

I'm a surging sea

my ocean welled up inside of me

when my time comes

I'll call my tide forth

my body then laid to rest on shore

when daybreak calls

my time to recede

back I'll call my waters

back inside of me

here they'll await the time

when again I'll release

this massive billow

swelling within me

today I feel loved

love returned

its energy creating intensity

much like steam propelling a ship

vapor causing mobility

your love generates power

gives me strength

allows my love to exist

today I feel love

today I feel loved

its power has overwhelmed me

To be with you

makes me more aware of myself

and the things surrounding me

you inspire me

There are some things

hard to say in words

hard to even understand

when sung in song

but the very same things

can be communicated in touch

your skin touching mine

tells me so much

Something about your touch

starts a spark

that rages into

a three alarm fire

It's the quiet time of my night

I think of you

visualize you

feel you

relive intimate times together

hold those thoughts

and lull myself to sleep

Boy could I tear your body up

with many teeny tiny caresses

strokes-nibbles-and sucks

my lips-tongue and even chin

cover you with every ounce

of affection I have left

then call on my reserve

to prolong it yet

Grey cloudy skies

seemingly ugly

bring me memories of beauty

beauty you gave to me

on just such a day

Waking to feel

the warmth of your body

very close to mine

is worth waking up for

and wonderful

to fall to sleep by

Sometimes you keep me waiting

anxiously anticipating

a call or maybe even

a visit from you

disappointments I've felt

anger withheld

always understanding

but with crush feelings felt

You've lost your initial excitement

expected I guess

but with what's left

I can't help worrying

Little things pile up

jealousies flare up

neurosis makes me believe

I'm losing you

I close myself off

you retaliate

closing yourself off from me

the gap grows

I could have cried

but tears wouldn't have

released me

would only make me feel worse

so I picked up my brush

and commenced my work

Sometimes I feel like a trophy

awarded to the winner

then put on a shelf

to rest on a pedestal

I love hard

make love softly

and hurt badly

Chapter Two

Can I Touch You

Can I touch you

with my life

bring you joy

with the tender moments

I wish to spend

beside you

lighten your burden

with this joy

I wish to share

with you

because you

have brought me joy

merely being you

enlightening me

with your refreshing

warmth and sensitivity

all too rare

in this life

but such an

outstanding ingredient

please don't ever lose it

Can I touch you

spend long hours

communicating these feelings

and sharing yours

with you

Please let me

touch you sweetheart

for you have

touched me

and I continuously feel you

and for that reason

I have found

a blessing in you

that doubles my determination

to remain "warmth" too

May I touch

your heart

vital organ

upon organ

making music

seeking rainbows

simply enjoying

sensations too often

not shared

something with someone

so very special

an experience

much too rare

don't let us

neglect this

something too beautiful

to lose

making music

seeking rainbows

and sensations

simply enjoying

not forsaking

love's refreshment

but touching this

revitalizing invigoration

beginning with

what we already have

it's all new

You're my kitten

so soft

so cuddly

and oh

so very warm

I feel your heat

so radiant

even from afar

your sensitive purr

excites me

even in my dreams

and how I love to

caress, pet and play

with your wild thick

yet glistening fur

to pamper

and care for you

brings me great joy

not to speak of

the thrill I feel

just seeing you

frisky, carefree

and completely happy

You're a warm

and sensitive gift

from above

and within

who recognized

my needs immediately

and understood

for you saw

"you" in me

as I see

"me" in you

reflections of

a mutual thirst

for all that is creativity

and all the desired space

for loving

and living

When I dream of you

it's always in Technicolor

your brightness transcends anything

two-dimensional

but also blacks

whites and grays

you're a peacock

I'm your admiration

you enlighten

and brighten

every day

as if in a painting

your varnish is a gloss

and a finishing protection

you're the fine print

and every decoration

but too

you exhaust not

even in thought

you're always there

a determining factor

even if your choice

may be silence

you're heard in an uproar

you're demonstrative

you're illustrative

it's not your choice

you reflect more

than any sunbeam

any full moon

any painted queen

you can't change it

it's your gift supreme

even though you

may not be

keenly aware of it

it's not added

it's just a part

of what is you

please let me

cherish and touch

all that is you

I love hard

make love softly

and hurt badly

Chapter Three

Whirlwind Love

There's no time

like the present

to laugh

to love

and live

there's no time

like the present

for us to share

love, laughter

and an occasional tear

there's no time

like the present

to give of ourselves

so that we might

feel and share

all life has to offer

there's no time

like the present

to live

Along came you

you reawakened

my spirit

when you

rekindled my fire

along came you

Am I slipping

or just falling

very comfortably

in love

I'll always remember

your first bright smile

your personal kiss

of sunshine

Something magnetic occurred

did I touch you

with my spirit

as you simultaneously

touched my soul

When you touched my hair

I felt you

and hoped

I'd get to feel you longer

the next time we met

and that night

we met again

in my dreams

The moon that you are

is a bright shining star

a full sphere

steering passions

and desires

illuminating the skies

with your heavens

Tossing

turning

dreaming

thinking

and wishing

Lightning struck

when first we touched

then thunder applauded

our very first kiss

We touch

we kiss

we love

then touch

kiss and love

over and over

till dawning

Good mornings

good afternoons

good evenings

and you give me

good nights too

Our love

the melting passions

of two bodies intertwined

the desire never

to get up

the smoldering thoughts

when we're apart

and the excitement

that makes us rush

to melt into

our passions again

our love

I'm happy again

life seems

even more beautiful

I'm myself again

heartfelt smiles have become

part of my existence

so naturally

my body's relaxed

my mind's at peace

and even just waking up

in the morning

causes me excitement

anticipations of painting

of writing

meeting and discovering

new people

new places

rediscovery shared with someone

special like you

I'm spoiled

by your warmth

your flame

your actions

and your caresses

My precious fawn

so fragile

but expressive

so strong

yet gentle

you can't blame people

for loving you

and caring so much

that they just want to protect you

from any and everything

that may hurt you

Can I love you

even if at times

it's from a distance

will you appear

to touch me at times

to show me you still care

will you always handle

my love with care

I'm thinking about you today

with warm thoughts

warm desires

in anticipation of

soft kisses

tender caresses

and eager passions

Whirlwind love

the soft caress

of a gentle

sea breeze

whirlwind love

torrential

I love hard

make love softly

and hurt badly

Chapter Four

A Butterfly's Dream

Your name should be Sunshine

sun shining

your rays set aglow warmth

that's golden with delight

your glow beckons

and keeps fires growing

with sizzling thoughts

and burning desires

can I call you Sunshine

I awoke this morning

with the desire

to see your reflection

beside mine

with the desire

to squeeze your

loving body

tightly to mine

while we kissed

our good morning greeting

then I felt

the sweet glow

of our union

growing stronger

wasn't I happy

upon finding a friend

in you

am I not now ecstatic

being able to

love you too

I awoke this morning

and wasn't I feeling you

hope you sensed it

and felt me too

I awoke

in the middle

of the night

to the sound

of your smile

You've grown on me

you're flowering

becoming more beautiful

with each passing day

bringing more

sunshine and light

as you open up to me

a flower very bright

containing all your

wondrous and beautiful treasures

as I rest on your petal

With morning's light

I opened my medicine cabinet

to find our toothbrushes

in their own mad

and intimate embrace

kissing

Love is

touching you

and feeling you

respond

When I say I love you

I mean I care

that the things in your life

most desired

don't remain merely dreams

that as often as possible

I'll be able to see you smiling

and know that

your smile is a reflection

of the happiness you feel inside

that all the ingredients needed

in your recipe

are in ample supply

in reach

when I say I love you

I mean I care

There are those times

when I imagine

but feel your mouth finding

then pressing against mine

so intensely

while your tongue seeks

then finds mine

so passionately mesmerized

in their own tangling

and intimate embraces

they have a mind all their own

until I feel your body

melting into mine

and your power

then I submit to

all that you give me

Sometimes I feel

like a butterfly

unable to fly

waiting for this

moisture to dry

from the tears

I've cried

weighing down my wings

my vision blurred

impairing the colors

of the rainbows

laying in wait before me

a butterfly crawling

and stumbling

waiting to fly

see clearly once again

through the pain

these years have caused me

There are no proven answers

to the questions of love

honesty can cause

just as much retreat

as deceit can

Was that only last week

when the clouds weren't

high enough to contain me

when I was so in love

everything was magic

or was it all merely a dream

a butterfly's dream

Our lives and dreams

sometimes tarnished by reality

Can we go to the ballet

and fall in love once again

I love hard

make love softly

and hurt badly

www.ingramcontent.com/pod-product-compliance
Lightning Source LLC
Chambersburg PA
CBHW061755040426
42447CB00011B/2313